Art & Activities for Kids

Make Sculptures!

Kim Solga

Cincinnati, Ohio

This hardcover edition of *Make Sculptures!* features a "self-jacket" that
eliminates the need for a separate dust jacket. It provides sturdy pro-
tection for your book while it saves paper, trees and energy.

96 95 94 93 92   5 4 3 2 1

Library of Congress Cataloging in Publication Data

Solga, Kim.
    Make Sculptures! / Kim Solga.
        p.   cm.—(Art & activities for kids)
    Summary: Photos and step-by-step instructions for eleven sculpture
projects for children aged six to eleven to make using clay, papier-
mâché, and household materials.
    ISBN 0-89134-420-9
    1. Paper sculpture—Juvenile literature. 2. Sculpture—Juvenile liter-
ature. 3. Modeling—Juvenile literature. 4. Found objects (Art)—Juvenile literature. [1. Sculpture—Technique. 2. Handicraft.] I. Title. II.
Series.
TT870.S63   1992
745.592—dc20
                                                    91-37354
                                                      CIP
                                                       AC

Edited by Julie Wesling Whaley
Design Direction by Clare Finney
Art Direction by Kristi Kane Cullen
Photography by Pamela Monfort
Very special thanks to Laryn Alcorn, Lori Bessenbacher, Sara Cherlin,
Laura Christianson, Susan Christianson, Shelley Edelschick, Carrie
Fogus, Seta Rusinak, Kathy Savage-Hubbard, Essena Setaro, Maya
Small, Niki Smith, Rose Speicher, Greg Statt, Felice Steele, and
Rachel Steele.

JUN 1993

Make Sculptures! features eleven unique sculpting projects plus numerous variations that will fire the imaginations of boys and girls aged six to eleven. The projects are open-ended: kids learn techniques they can use to produce sculptures of their own design.

By inviting kids to try new things, *Make Sculptures!* encourages individual creativity. Each project has a theme stated at the very beginning. Children will learn (subtly) about architecture and design, additive and subtractive sculpture, collage and assemblage, and art forms ranging from clay pots to pop art. They'll use their artistic, fine motor and problem-solving skills to produce beautiful finished sculptures. All the projects are kid-tested to ensure success and inspire confidence.

But the emphasis of *Make Sculptures!* is on fun. Kids will love experimenting with such diverse mediums as paper, clay, plastic, papier maché, twigs, textiles, plaster and various found objects.

Getting the Most out of the Projects

While the projects provide clear step-by-step instructions and photographs, children should feel free to substitute and improvise. Some of the projects are easy to do in a short amount of time. Others require more patience and even adult supervision. The symbols on page 6 will help you recognize the more challenging activities.

The list of materials shown at the beginning of each activity is for the featured project only. Suggested alternatives may require different supplies. Again, children are encouraged to substitute and use whatever materials they have access to (and permission to use!). The projects offer flexibility to make it easy for you and your child to try as many activities as you wish.

Safety

The activities in this book were developed for the enjoyment of children. We've taken every precaution to ensure their safety and success. Please follow the directions and note where an adult's help is required. In fact, feel free to work alongside your young artists as often as you can. They will appreciate help in reading and learning new techniques, and will love the chance to talk with you and show off their creations. Children thrive on attention and praise, and art adventures are the perfect setting for both.

Collecting Supplies

All of the projects can be done with household items or inexpensive, easy-to-find supplies (see page 7 for definitions of any craft materials you're not already familiar with). Here are some household items you'll want to make sure you have on hand: newspapers, scrap paper and cloth, cardboard tubes from paper towels or wrapping paper, old hardware and interesting "stuff," plastic cups, plastic utensils, flour, masking tape, duct tape, electrical tape, glue, wire, twine, bucket and sponges.

4

Be a Good Artist

Work Habits

Get permission to work at your chosen workspace before you begin. Cover your workspace with newspaper or a vinyl tablecloth.

Wear a smock or big, old shirt to protect your clothes whenever you work with something messy!

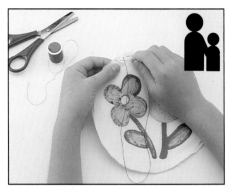

Follow the directions carefully for each project. When you see the adult and child symbol, have an adult help you.

Don't put art materials in your mouth. If you're working with a younger child, don't let him put art materials in his mouth, either.

The clock symbol means you must wait to let something dry before going on to the next step. It is very important not to rush ahead.

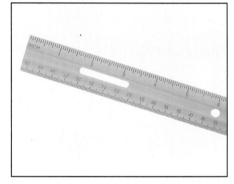

This symbol, ″, means inches— 12″ means 12 inches; cm means centimeter (3 cm equal about 1″).

Collect things you can use to make interesting sculptures: shells, hardware, cardboard tubes, little toys, and stuff like feathers and sequins.

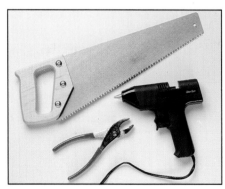

If you want to use a small saw to make Air Towers, a pliers for Funky Junk, or a hot glue gun, get an adult to help you.

Sweep up scraps and clean up splatters and spills as soon as they happen. Always finish by cleaning your workspace and all your tools.

Art Terms

Sculpture. When you build a sculpture, your work isn't flat, like a drawing or painting. It's three-dimensional art—a sculpture goes up and out; it is thick and tall and round. Some sculptures stand on their own. Others hang from the wall. They're all fun to build and look at!

Plaster of Paris is a powder you can buy at a hardware store or art supply store. You mix it with water to make a white plaster that dries hard.

In Soft Stone Sculpture, you mix plaster of Paris with *vermiculite*, a type of soil you can buy at garden stores. The vermiculite will keep the plaster soft for a longer time so you can carve it easily. Vermiculite comes in different forms. The kind that looks ground up works better than the flaky kind but either one is fine to use.

Papier maché is a kind of sculpture using newspaper or paper towel strips and a simple paste. You can use wallpaper paste, or you can make your own paste with white flour. Using a blender works best, but you can mix the paste by hand (see page 38).

Clay. A recipe for making sculpting dough is on page 30. You can also buy different kinds of clay at craft and art supply stores. Some dry in the air, others require baking, and others never get very hard so you can reuse them.

Glue. Most of the projects in this book can be done with regular white glue. For projects where you use cloth, *fabric glue* works better because it's specially made for cloth. *Carpenter's glue* from a hardware store works best on heavy things like metal and wood.

To speed up the projects that need glue, *ask an adult* to help you use a *glue gun*. You can buy them at craft stores and supermarkets. Glue guns melt plastic glue sticks, and you squeeze the hot glue where you need it. It cools almost instantly and holds things tight. Since the glue is hot, you must always be very careful.

Tape. *Masking tape* is fine for most of the projects in this book that call for tape. *Clear adhesive tape* works well for paper projects. *Duct tape* or *electrical tape* works best on plastic and metal.

Paint. If you want to paint some of your sculptures after you build them, use *tempera* paint or *acrylic* paint. Both clean up easily with water. Tempera paint works well on most surfaces; acrylic is better on plastic, metal, and clay. *Fabric paint* is best for cloth. Get an adult to help you use fabric paint, and follow the instructions on the label.

Permanent markers and **fabric crayons** are other things you can use to decorate your cloth sculptures. *Always have an adult help you* use them correctly.

Varnish will add a shiny, waterproof finish to your sculpture. *Always have an adult help you* brush on varnish or acrylic gloss medium after your sculpture and paint are completely dry.

Theme Sculptures

Assemblage

Turn your favorite collection into a work of art! Gather seashells at the beach or a box of treasures from around the house. Any group of objects that go together will make a wonderful theme sculpture.

Materials needed:

Found objects

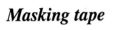

Masking tape

Felt pen

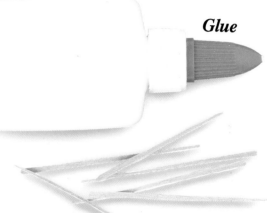

Glue

Plastic or wood base

Toothpicks

1 Pick a couple of large items to go on the bottom. Arrange them so they balance and are sturdy. Use the pen to mark where they touch.

2 Use a toothpick to spread glue over your marks. Put things back together, holding each one in place until the glue starts to dry.

3 Add more little stuff. Use masking tape to hold things in place until the glue dries. You may need several work sessions to finish.

8

Toy Sculpture

Forest Sculpture

Seashell Sculpture

9

Stuffings

Soft Sculpture

You can make soft sculpture people, animals, toys and pillows—it's easy! Start with cloth or paper. Decorate with paint, crayons or markers. Then staple, sew or glue it together. Stuffing makes your sculpture come to life. You can even sculpt yourself or a friend! (Use big paper like butcher paper or kraft paper.)

Tempera paint

Materials needed:

Glue and clear tape

Marker

Decorations

1 Put two layers of big paper on the floor. One person lays down. Another person traces around him.

2 Color the tracing with markers, paint or crayons. Add details to make it look like the real person!

3 Fasten the two sheets of paper together with a few staples. Cut the person out, both layers of paper at once. Save the scraps.

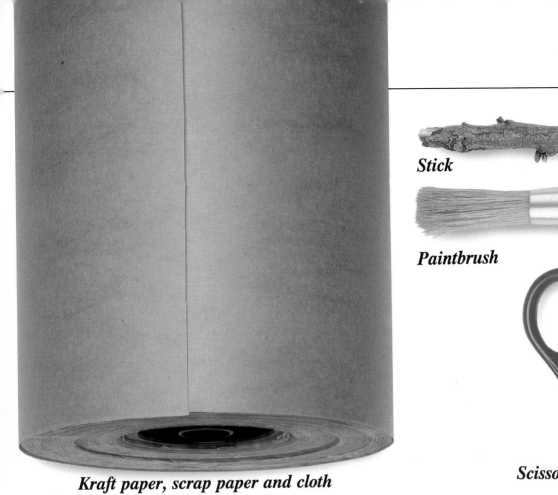

Kraft paper, scrap paper and cloth

Stick

Paintbrush

Scissors

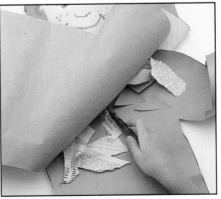

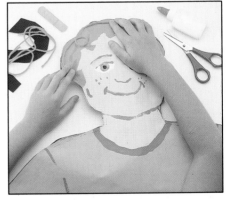

Stapler and staples

4 Staple around the head — put the staples very close together. Stuff scraps of paper inside. Staple another small area and stuff it.

5 Use a stick to stuff paper scraps into hard-to-reach places. Use tape to patch any rips. When it's stuffed full, staple the last opening.

6 Add decorations! Cut yarn for hair, fringe paper for eyelashes, glue on beads, buttons or sequins.

Paper Stuffings

Make a stuffed rocket or some other toy.

Don't feed the paper cat or fish— they're stuffed already!

These kids have lots of fun decorations. Do you see felt numbers? A real button? A bandage? A necklace? Sequins? Yarn? A real jump rope? A fabric bow?

Fabric Stuffings

1 Make a soft sculpture pillow! First, draw a design on paper: a circle, square, or simple animal shape will be easy to sew and stuff.

2 Pin two layers of cloth together and cut out the shape you drew. Copy your design onto one of the cut pieces with fabric paint or permanent markers.

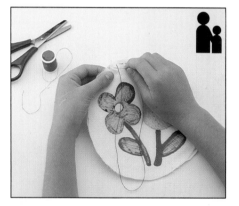

3 Put the colored cloth and the other piece together with the colored design facing in. Have an adult help you sew almost all the way around the pillow.

4 Turn the pillow right side out. Stuff it with newspaper or scraps of cloth (or puffy fiberfill from a sewing store for a really comfy pillow).

5 When the pillow is stuffed full, stitch the last bit closed. Be careful with the sharp needle! Ask for help if you need it.

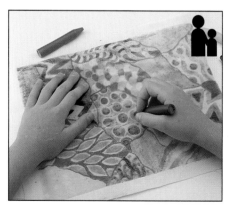

6 You can also draw on the cloth with regular crayons, and have an adult iron your picture between sheets of paper to make the crayon melt into the fabric.

If you don't like to sew, you can use fabric glue to put the two sides of your Fabric Stuffings together, but the edges may not look as neat.

Pillow colored with crayons

Painted bug with button eyes, wire antennae and pipe cleaner legs

Painted snake

Time Capsules

Collage Sculpture

Can you tell a story without using any words? These plastic sculptures let you describe a time or event that is special to you. Use pictures and objects you make and collect, and seal them in a capsule to save forever.

Materials needed:

Scissors

Glue

2 clear plastic cups

Stuff

1 Collect things to tell your story. Clip photos or make things from clay. Arrange them in one of the cups – it will be the bottom cup. Glue them in place if you wish.

2 To hang something in your capsule, tie or glue it onto a short piece of yarn. Then glue the yarn to the bottom of the other cup – it will be the top.

3 When your arrangement is finished, spread glue all around the rim of the bottom cup. Carefully set the top cup down into the glue to seal them together.

16

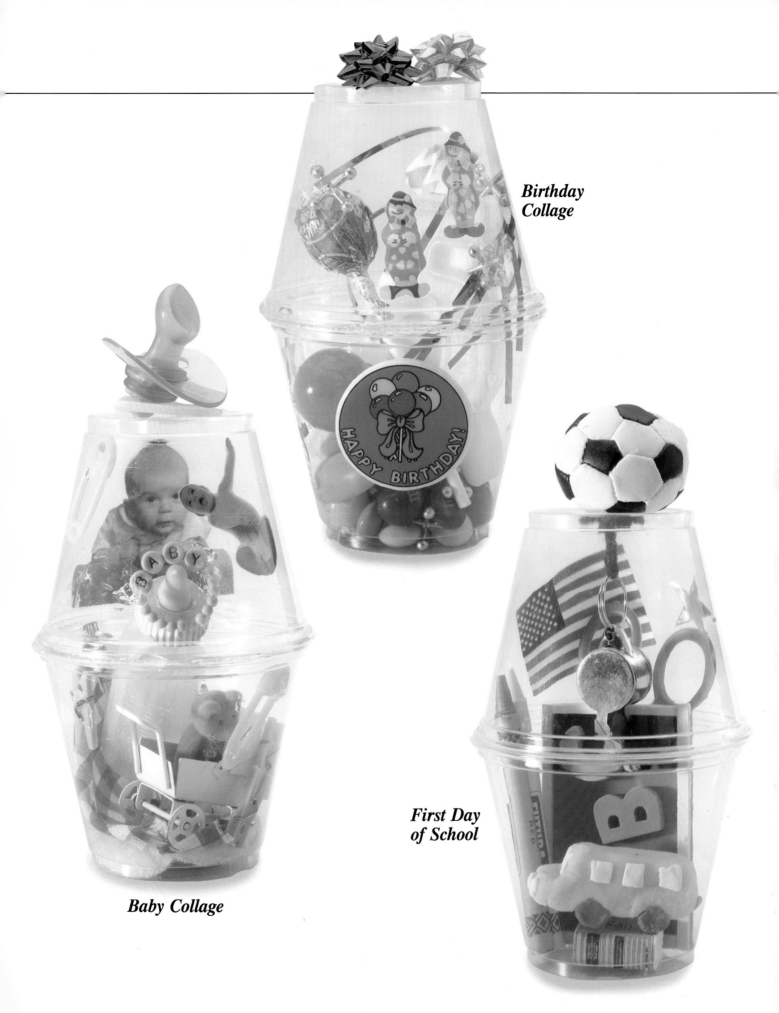

Birthday Collage

Baby Collage

First Day of School

17

Soft Stone Carving

Subtractive Sculpture

Sculptors cut into solid rock with strong tools, carving until the block of stone becomes a beautiful sculpture. When you mix plaster with vermiculite, your block of "stone" will stay soft for a long time—it's easy and fun to carve a sculpture of your own.

When you carve this mixture, use old tools. The plaster would ruin good, metal tools. *Never pour unused plaster down the drain.* Dump it right into the garbage. When you wash it off your hands, use lots and lots of water.

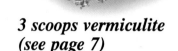

3 scoops vermiculite (see page 7)

Materials needed:

Spoon

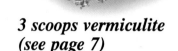

Nail

Stick

Milk carton

Paintbrush

1 Measure the vermiculite and plaster into the bucket. Stir it with a stick. Add about two scoops of water and stir until it looks like thick gravy.

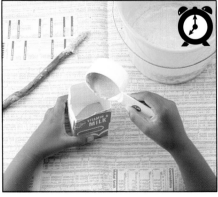

2 Pour the plaster into the milk carton. It will turn hard in about fifteen minutes. It will be ready to carve in a half hour.

3 When the half hour is up, peel away the milk carton. Little by little, scrape the plaster with the spoon to shape it. Work over newspaper to catch the scrapings.

18

Varnish

Bucket and water

Measuring scoop

1/4
CUP
60
ml

2 scoops plaster of Paris

Newspaper

Plastic bag

4 It may take time to get the shape you want. The plaster will stay soft for two or three days if you wrap it in a plastic bag when you stop to rest.

5 Use a nail to carve details into your sculpture. When you're finished, let it dry for two weeks.

6 You can have an adult help you brush varnish on your sculpture when it's completely dry. This will protect it and make it shine.

Soft Stone Sculptures

A sculpture of a head and shoulders is called a *bust*.

This sculpture is an *abstract*.

This apple was made with ground vermiculite mixed with plaster and water. The worm seems to like it!

Your sculpture might look like an ancient figure from far away.

20

This rabbit was made with flaky vermiculite mixed with plaster and water.

This whale was shaped in a plastic bag and then carved.

Modeling Stone

Another way of sculpting with plaster is to treat it like clay and mold it with your hands before you start to carve.

1 Follow the directions for mixing plaster in Step 1 on page 18. Pour it into a plastic bag. As it starts to harden, squeeze it into the main shape you want for your sculpture.

2 In about a half hour your plaster will be ready to carve. Take it out of the plastic bag and follow Steps 3 through 6 on pages 18 and 19.

Tube Towers

Architectural Sculpture

You'll become a real architect when you make these great tube towers. Learn how to connect tubes and support your tower as you build it higher and higher. Use ribbons, yarn, and colored paper to decorate your sculpture.

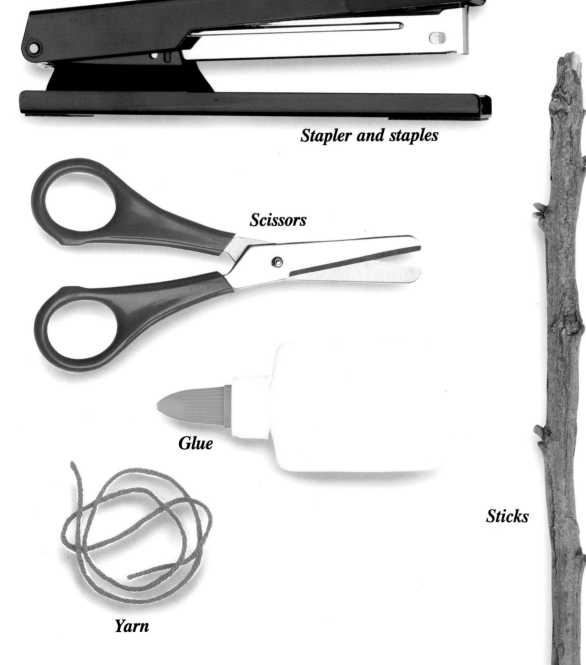

Materials needed:

Stapler and staples

Scissors

Glue

Yarn

Sticks

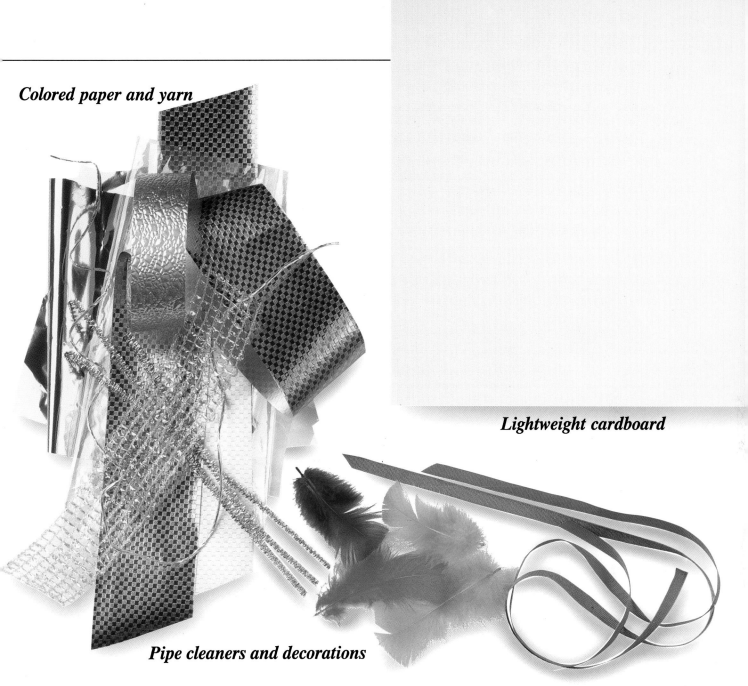

Colored paper and yarn

Lightweight cardboard

Pipe cleaners and decorations

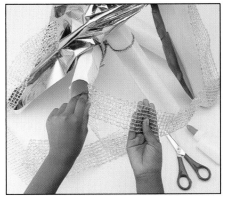

1 Make tubes by rolling cardboard and stapling the ends. Begin putting tubes together with tape or pipe cleaners.

2 Add tubes one at a time. Experiment with ways of putting them together so they'll stand up on their own and be sturdy.

3 When you finish building the tube tower, decorate it with fancy paper, ribbons, yarn and other bright decorations.

Air Towers

The shiny paper used to decorate this structure makes it look like a space station!

This pyramid is made with natural sticks. The yarn and decorations are woven all around. See pages 42 and 43 for another weaving project.

Sometimes it's just too nice to stay indoors. So make an Air Tower outside! Use long sticks or PVC pipes from the hardware store. Connect your tubes with masking tape, duct tape or twine. Work with friends to build your tower higher than your head!

Photo by Fred W. Smith

Fast Food Giants

Pop Art Sculpture

Celebrate your favorite food with a bigger-than-life-size sculpture! Make a pizza slice as big as a poster, or a fabric hot dog to use as a pillow. These fast food giants are more fun than a trip to the ice cream parlor!

Materials needed:

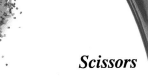

Scissors

Glue

Fabric glue

Decorations

Pizza

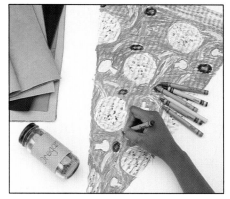

1 Design your giant food on paper. Gather paper, fabric, and decorations you can use to make it look real.

2 Cut a triangle or wedge shape out of cardboard. Cover it with brown paper. Roll up some paper to look like a crust and glue it in place.

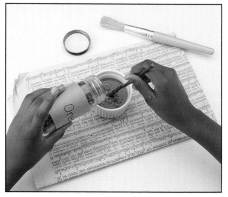

3 Mix real pizza spices or tea leaves with dark red paint to make pizza sauce! Paint it onto your cardboard triangle.

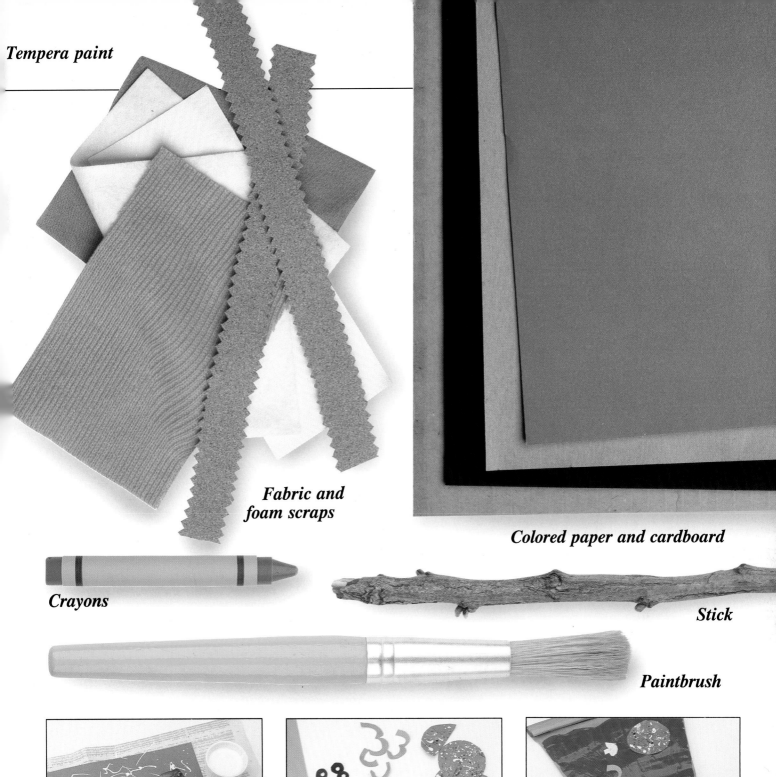

Tempera paint

Fabric and foam scraps

Colored paper and cardboard

Crayons

Stick

Paintbrush

4 To make pepperoni, splatter white, black, and brown paint on red paper with a stick or tooth-brush. Work over newspaper!

5 When the paint dries, cut out big pepperoni circles. Cut other toppings out of paper, too, like green peppers and black olives.

6 This pizza has fabric mush-rooms and cheese made of foam. Arrange the toppings and glue them onto the pizza slice.

27

Fast Food Feast

This cheery cherry pie has a crust made of rolled cork (from a craft store). The top crust was cut with a pinking shears. The middle is foam, covered with red fabric and pompons. A sprinkle of red glitter on top looks like cinnamon.

This hot dog is made from foam covered with old pantyhose! The bun is cloth-covered foam, the mustard is felt and the ketchup is a red shoelace.

Here's a painted cardboard ice cream cone. The scoop of ice cream is pink satin stuffed with puffy fiber from a craft store. Glitter paint drizzled on top makes it sparkly.

Critter Pots

Sculpting with Clay

It's fun to make little clay pots. It's fun to make statues of animals and birds. But the most fun of all is when you put them together to make critter pots! There are many kinds of clay and dough you can buy at art supply stores or toy stores. Or make your own with this recipe.

Sculpting Dough: Mix 4 cups flour, 1 cup salt, and 1¾ cups warm water in a bowl. Knead with your hands for 10 minutes. Divide up and add different food colors, if you want. Store in a plastic bag when you're not working with it.

Materials needed:

Varnish

Toothpicks

Acrylic paints

Waxed paper

Garlic press

Water

Cheese grater

Dull table knife and a paintbrush

1 Roll an egg-sized piece of clay into a ball. Make a hole in the middle with your thumb.

2 Pinch around and around to make a bowl. The sides of the bowl should be ¼″ (1 cm) thick.

3 Now make a critter! Make little balls to shape into heads and eyes. Roll little snakes and pinch them into legs and tails.

4 Cut flat slabs of clay. Trim and pinch them into the shapes of wings or ears.

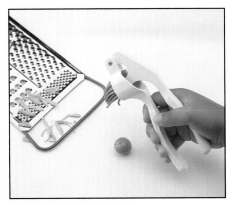

5 Use a garlic press or a cheese grater to make hair or fur, or straw for your animal to eat or sleep on.

6 Join pieces of clay together and rub their edges gently with your finger. Getting your finger wet will help make it smooth.

7 Use toothpicks to carve texture. Add details like teeth, toenails, and nostrils.

8 Let your sculpture air dry for a few days until it's hard. Paint it with acrylic paint — make it look real or silly.

9 Have an adult help you brush on a coat of varnish when the paint is dry. This will make it shiny and will help protect it.

Critter Pots

Elephant Pot

Lion Pot

Panda Pot

Pig Pot

Duck Pot

Frog Pot

33

Funky Junk

Additive Sculpture

Don't throw away that old junk! Be creative and turn it into original works of art. Invent new creatures with old machine parts, pieces of hardware, and used kitchen gadgets. Additive sculpture is a process of building and adding pieces as you create. The design is totally up to you — and your junk!

Scissors

Materials needed:

Wire

Electrical tape

Carpenter's glue

1 Take a good look at your junk — do you see a character waiting to be created? Hold one thing next to another until you see something you like.

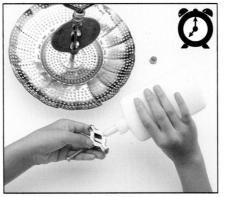

2 When you've found a good design, begin gluing pieces together. Build from the bottom up, working slowly and letting the glue dry as you go.

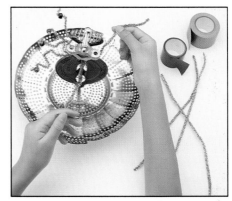

3 Wire or pipe cleaners help hold things in place. You could also use duct tape or electrical tape to hold things together and as part of your design.

Junk and decorations

Pipe cleaners

Duct tape

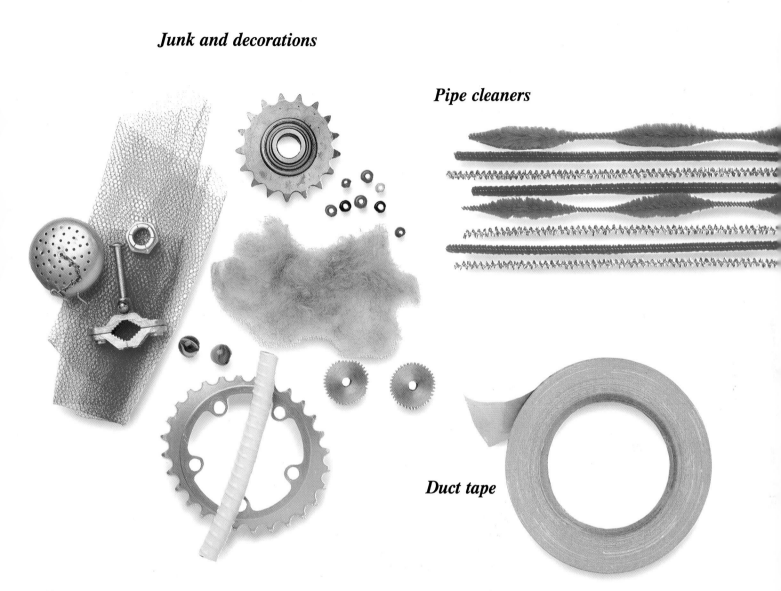

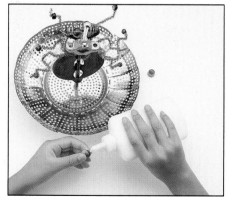

4 Once you've made the basic shape for your character, add decorations to give it life. Glue on wiggly eyes or eyes made of beads or marbles.

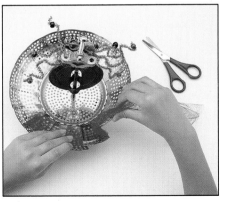

5 Yarn or cotton puffs make great hair. Make clothes out of scraps of cloth or aluminum foil. Bend thin wire to make eyeglasses.

6 Add beads, feathers, and decorations. Cut things out of paper. You decide when your funky junk creature is finished.

Funky Junk

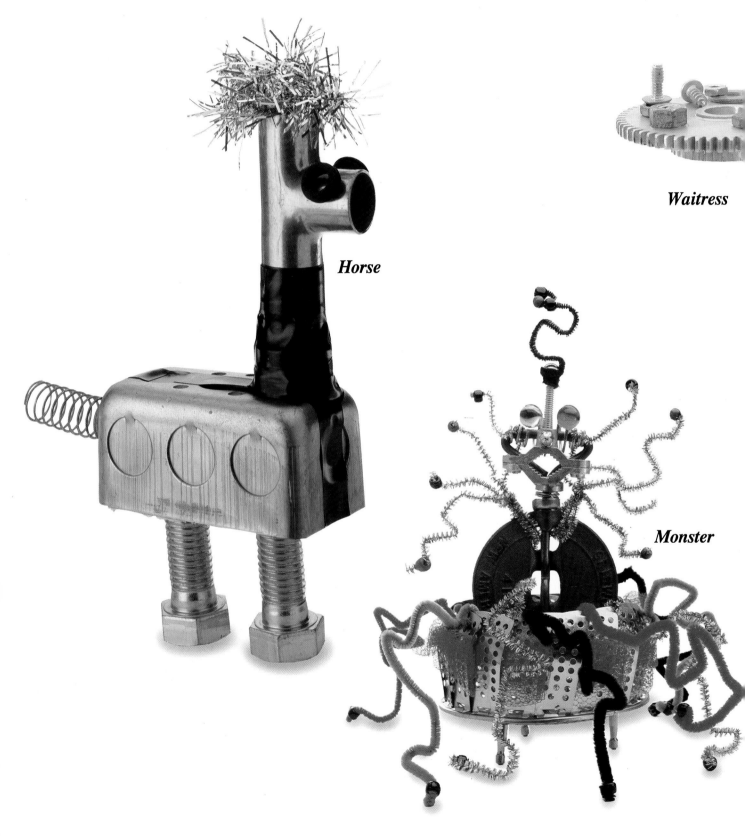

Horse

Waitress

Monster

Lady Robot

Sunflower Guy

Papier Maché Animals

Sculpting with Papier Maché

You can make big, bright sculptures with a simple process called *papier maché*. It's easy, but it takes a long time. You'll need to put on three layers of paper and paste to make it strong. And you have to wait a day in between each layer to let it dry!

Papier maché can be messy—but it doesn't have to be. Wear old clothes and work over newspaper. Throw leftover paste in the garbage, not down the drain. Wipe excess paste off your hands with paper towels before washing them, and use lots of water when you wash.

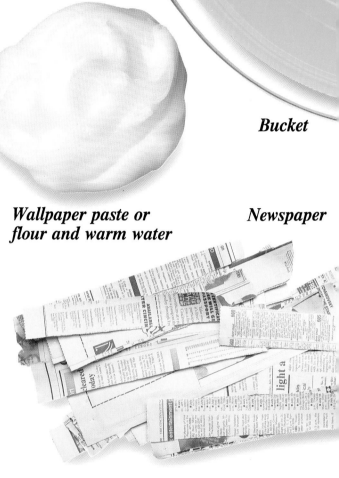

Bucket

Wallpaper paste or flour and warm water

Newspaper

Materials needed:

Paper tubes

Paintbrush

1 Build the body of an animal. Crumple newspaper and hold it together with masking tape. Use paper plates, boxes and tubes.

2 Use wallpaper paste, or use your hands to mix 2 cups water and 1 cup of flour in the bucket to make a smooth, thick paste.

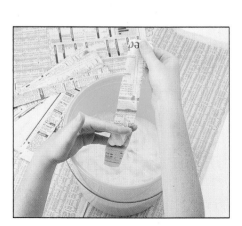

3 Cut or tear newspaper into strips. Dip a strip into the paste and gently pull it through your fingers to rub off extra paste.

Masking tape

Paper towels

Tempera or acrylic paint

Varnish

Small boxes

4 Lay the sticky newspaper strip on the animal frame and smooth it down with your fingers. Use lots of strips and paste to hold the body pieces together.

5 Let the first layer dry overnight. Then add another layer of paper strips and paste. Let it dry overnight. Make a third layer using paper towel strips.

6 Let the third layer dry overnight. Then paint it. Copy a photograph to make your animal look real. Or use bright colors to make a fancy beast.

Papier Maché Zoo

Colorful Turtle

When your papier maché animal is dry, have an adult help you spread on a coat of acrylic varnish. This will protect your work and make it shine.

Elephant Calf

Orange Tabby Cat

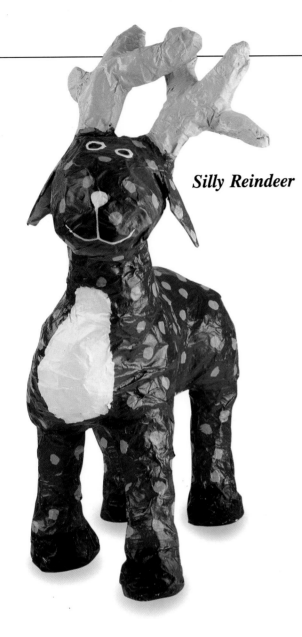

Silly Reindeer

Your papier maché animals can be small toys or almost life-size decorations for your room, like this baby giraffe.

Wild Alligator

Pinto Horse

41

Twig Weavings

Textile Art

Everyone knows that you can weave cloth, but have you ever tried to weave sticks? It's easy to turn pretty driftwood or twigs into beautiful wall sculptures with *textiles*: yarn, fabric and soft materials.

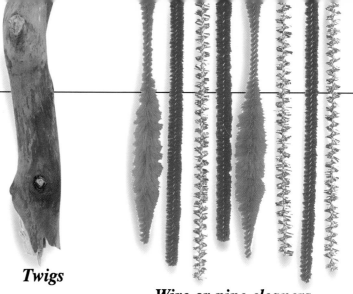

Twigs

Wire or pipe cleaners

Materials needed:

Scissors

Decorations

Yarn and cloth scraps

1 Lay your sticks side by side. Twist the pipe cleaners across the middle, going in and out around each stick. Make a loop in the back (for hanging).

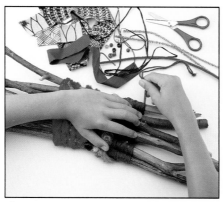

2 Cut long pieces of yarn or fabric. Weave with them one at a time. Tie each one to an outside stick and go in and out between the sticks.

3 Push the rows close together as you weave. Each time you get to the end of a cut piece, tie it to an outside stick and trim the end short. Add decorations.

Finished Weaving

Wrap rope and yarn around single sticks and use them for drumsticks! Decorate a cardboard oatmeal container to make a drum.

Fantastic Faces

Paper Sculpture

Masks are made by artists all over the world. People use them in plays, dances, parades and parties. You can make fantastic faces to hang on the wall or make a mask to wear by cutting out eye holes. Staple the face to a paper plate for extra strength (cut eye holes in the paper plate, too!). Make the faces shown here, or design your own.

Materials needed:

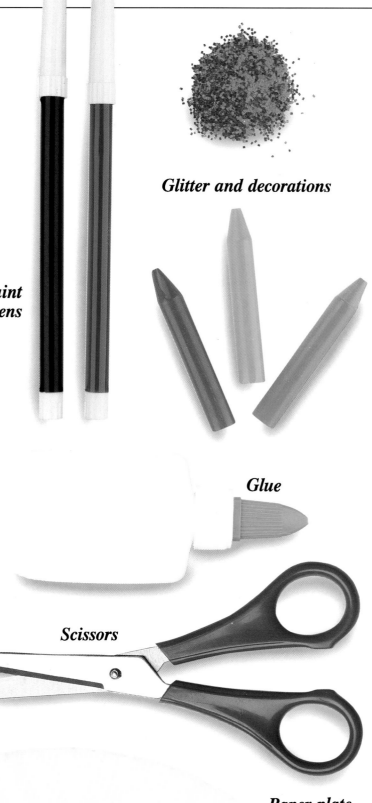

Crayons, paint or felt pens

Glitter and decorations

Colored paper

Foil

Glue

Scissors

Paper plate

Bumps

1 Make a circle of paper and then cut into the middle. Spread glue along one edge of the cut.

2 Overlap the other edge of the cut and hold it in place until the glue sets.

3 To glue it onto the face, spread glue along just the bottom of the bump and set it in place.

Nose

1 Use a bump for an animal nose. For a human nose, fold a scrap of paper in half and cut a shape like the side of a nose.

2 Unfold it and trim until it looks good. You can cut, glue, and overlap the bottom to make it stand up a little.

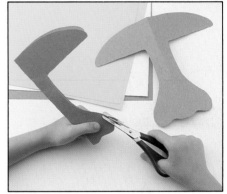

3 To add eyebrows, fold a scrap of paper in half and cut a shape like this. Unfold and trim it (see the African Mask on the next page).

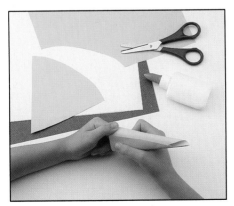

Cone. Cut a wedge of paper and spread glue along one edge. Roll the paper into an ice cream cone shape and hold it until the glue sets.

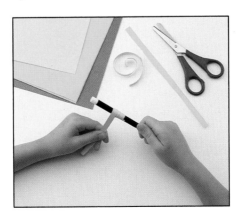

Curl. Cut a skinny strip of paper and wrap it around a pen. Hold it tight for a minute, then unwrap it and it will stay curly.

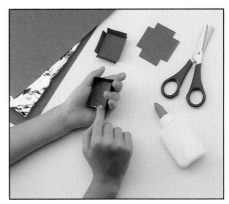

Box. Cut a piece of paper into a kind of cross shape as shown. Fold each side up and put glue on the edges (see the Robot Mask on page 47).

Masks and Faces

Twine for hair

Sequins make it sparkle

Little Girl Face

Curls for hair

Cut out the eyes
for a mask

Layers of paper
for decoration

Cut a fringe
for eyelashes

African Mask

Folded paper
cut to look like lace

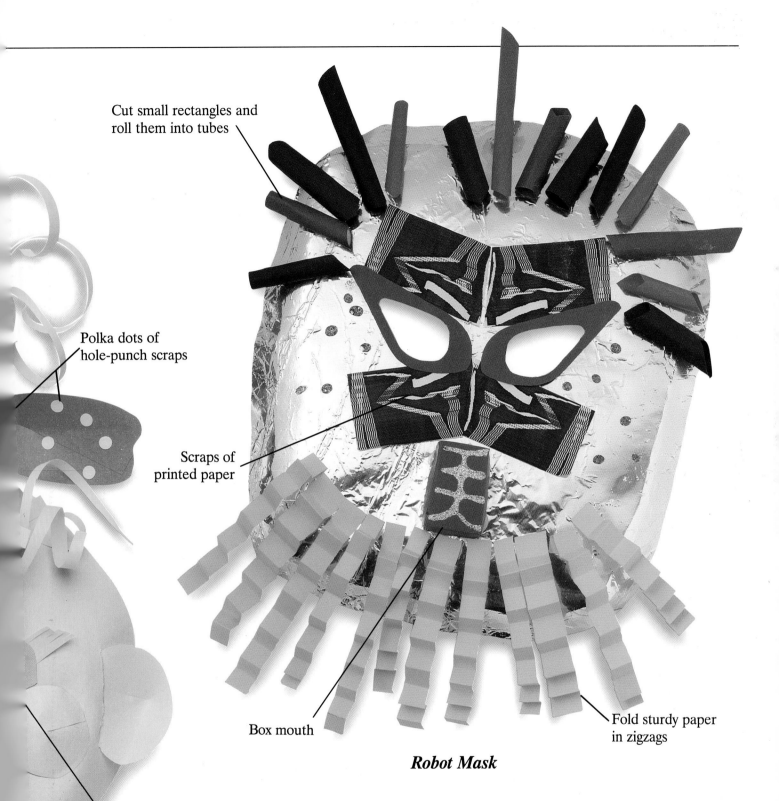

Cut small rectangles and
roll them into tubes

Polka dots of
hole-punch scraps

Scraps of
printed paper

Box mouth

Fold sturdy paper
in zigzags

Flat eyes—layers of paper for
eyeball, iris, and sparkle

Robot Mask

Friendly Faces

Cut slits to fit the
ears into the head

Cut a jagged edge for fur

Cut a V up into the bump
to make a snout

Bear Cub

Cut a fringe for feathers

Bumps for eyes with a tiny,
white triangle sparkle

Cone with the end pinched
flat for a beak

Plywood stick for a handle ——— **Bird Face**